POLAR BEARS

by Sophie Lockwood

Content Adviser: Barbara E. Brown, Associate, Mammal Division, The Field Museum, Chicago, IL

THE CHILD'S WORLD®, CHANHASSEN, MINNESOTA

POLAR BEARS

Published in the United States of America by The Child's World®
PO Box 326 • Chanhassen, MN 55317-0326 • 800-599-READ • www.childsworld.com

Acknowledgements:

The Child's World®: Mary Berendes, Publishing Director

Editorial Directions, Inc.: E. Russell Primm, Editorial Director; Pam Rosenberg, Editor; Judith Shiffer, Assistant Editor; Matt Messbarger, Editorial Assistant; Susan Hindman, Copy Editor; Emily Dolbear, Proofreader; Judith Frisbie and Olivia Nellums, Fact Checkers; Tim Griffin/IndexServ, Indexer; Cian Loughlin O'Day, Photo Researcher, Linda S. Koutris, Photo Editor

The Design Lab: Kathleen Petelinsek, Designer, Production Artist, and Cartographer

Photos:

Cover: Getty Images/The Image Bank/Wayne R. Bilenduke; half title/CIP: Corbis; frontispiece: Getty Images/The Image Bank/Grant Faint.

Interior: Animals Animals/Earth Scenes: 11 (Johnny Johnson), 24 (Daniel A. Bedell), 34 (Richard Kolar); Corbis: 8 (Staffan Widstrand), 12 (Dan Guravish), 22 (Werner Forman); Getty Images/Photodisc/Pat Powers/Cherryl Schafer: 5-bottom right and 30; Getty Images/Stone: 5-top left and 7 (James Balog), 32 (Wayne R. Bilenduke); Photodisc: 5-top right and 15, 5-bottom left and 37, 29; Norbert Rosing/Animals Animals/Earth Scenes: 5-middle left and 19, 16.

Library of Congress Cataloging-in-Publication Data

Lockwood, Sophie.
  Polar bears / by Sophie Lockwood.
    p. cm. — (The world of mammals)
  Includes index.
  ISBN 1-59296-501-6 (lib. bdg. : alk. paper) 1. Polar bear—Juvenile literature. I. Title.
II. World of mammals (Chanhassen, Minn.)
  QL737.C27L63 2005
  599.786—dc22   2005000537

TABLE OF CONTENTS

Chapter One

Nanuk

On the Canadian **tundra,** the Inuit and the polar bear share a bond that reaches back thousands of years. The Inuit depended on *nanuk,* the polar bear, to help them survive in the frigid north.

Nanuk was the most valued animal hunted by the Inuit. Native people respected the polar bear for its hunting skills and ability to live in such a harsh land. They saw the bears as wise, powerful, nearly human creatures. According to legend, Nanuk lived as a human when in his own home. He shed his thick fur coat, walked on two legs, and talked like a man.

In early times, polar bear hunts were long, difficult events. The bears roamed over a wide territory. An Inuit hunter expected to spend several days on the hunt. The Arctic weather posed serious

Would You Believe?
The only part of the polar bear the Inuit didn't use was the liver. Polar bear liver contains so much vitamin A that eating it would make humans very sick.

*A modern Inuit hunter poses with his hunting rifle. The Inuit
have hunted polar bears for thousands of years.*

Polar bear skins can be used to make many items such as blankets, boots, and pants.

threats: brutal cold, endless winds, and gusting snows. When the hunter finally located his prey, he speared it with a harpoon.

The hunter showed respect for his prey. He hung the polar bear's skin on his lodge wall for several days. He placed knives and bow drills by the skin of a male bear and needle cases and skin scrapers beside a female bear's skin. The Inuit believed that offering tools showed respect to the polar bear's soul, or *tatkok.* They hoped that the bear's soul would tell other bears of such honors. Then, other bears would be willing to be killed by a man to receive such respect.

Inuit, like most native people, made use of the entire catch. The Inuit ate the polar bear's meat. They sucked oil from the bones. Bear skins made blankets, boots, pants, and tunics. **Sinew** became sewing thread, and thin bones became needles. The Inuit strung bear teeth to make bracelets and necklaces. They turned heavy bones into excellent tools. They processed the bear's thick layer of fat to make grease or tallow. Nothing usable was wasted.

To the Inuit, polar bears represent the spirit of the north. Inuit legends of the great "ice bear" pass from generation to generation. The Inuit and the polar bear continue to share the land of the midnight sun.

Chapter Two

Hunting on the Ice Pack

A polar bear sow and her two cubs move out onto the **pack ice.** The mother's keen sense of smell helps her locate a ringed seal's birthing den. The cubs are learning a valuable lesson: finding and catching food.

Ringed seals build caves under snowdrifts on the Arctic pack ice. The mother bear sniffs above a possible cave. She smells a seal pup under the ice. Now it's time for true hunting skill. Mother rears up on her hind legs and pounces down hard to break through the cave roof. She needs three pounces to reach the pup. The hunt is a success. Today, the sow and her cubs eat well.

Male polar bears, called boars, use different hunting methods from mothers with cubs. They stalk or still-hunt their prey. Stalking takes place when seals leave the water and rest on ice floes. The polar

Would You Believe?
The Arctic **ice pack** has two unusual water features: leads and polynyas. Leads are open waterways or cracks between fields of pack ice. Polynyas, open water areas that are surrounded by ice and never freeze over, are formed by winds or currents.

bear boar swims along leads or walks across ice to its prey. He sneaks up on the seal and grabs it.

Still-hunting, the most common type of hunting, requires patience. Females without cubs and males usually still-hunt to catch prey. Seals, whales, and walruses must breathe every few minutes. They rise at polynyas, open water areas that never freeze over. A polar bear simply lies

A polar bear and her cubs hunt for their next meal. Female polar bears must teach their cubs how to hunt before the cubs can survive on their own.

still by a breathing hole and waits. When the prey pops up to breathe, the bear uses its claws or teeth to haul its catch from the water.

THE PERFECT WINTER COAT

Polar bears have the perfect winter coat. Their dense fur has two layers. The first layer is thick and waterproof. The outer layer appears to be white but is not. Outer hair shafts are clear and hollow. They look white because they reflect light off the snow. Depending on the angle of the sun, a polar bear's coat may look white, yellow, or even light tan.

A young, male polar bear hunts at a breathing hole.

After swimming, bears shake off water to keep their fur waterproof. Snow makes an excellent towel. Often, polar bears rub their fur in snow to get dry.

Only a polar bear's nose and footpads are black. The rest of the animal's surface is white. Feet measure 36 centimeters (12 inches) across. Only partially covered by hair, the feet have nubs of skin on the bottom for traction on ice, much like nonslip bedroom slippers. Front paws, with their sharp claws, provide powerful weapons when hunting and fighting. Polar bear claws, like those of all bears, are not retractable—they can't be pulled in and hidden.

Paws also help bears paddle in the water. Polar bears are powerful swimmers and can easily swim 160 kilometers (100 miles) in the course of a day. Interestingly, they are the only four-legged mammals that use only their front limbs for swimming. Polar bears can dive and remain underwater for up to two minutes. Their nostrils close under water.

THE POLAR BEAR'S BODY

A polar bear has a longer neck than other bears. Its head is also smaller and flatter than the heads of other kinds of bears.

A polar bear needs a keen sense of smell to survive in the Arctic. It is the most important sense when hunting

for prey. Research shows that polar bears have the best sense of smell of all bears. They can smell a seal that is 32 kilometers (20 mi) away. When testing new or strange items, a polar bear touches them with its nose.

A polar bear's hearing and sight are equal to those of humans. One difference in polar bear vision is a thin skin over each eye. Scientists think this skin acts like sunglasses. It protects the bear's vision from strong light reflected off the snow and ice. Another difference between polar bear and human vision is that polar bears can see colors even when it is dark.

Polar bears suffer from a strange problem considering where they live. They often overheat—even at temperatures far below freezing. This is because the polar bear body has three layers to keep it warm: 10 centimeters (4 in) of blubber, a tough hide, and thick fur.

Surprisingly, a polar bear's coat is so thick and so effective that almost no heat escapes from the bear's body. Scientists tried an experiment. They took pictures of polar bears with an **infrared** camera. Infrared photos show heat, yet the polar bear picture came out blank. The only heat that escaped from the bears' bodies was their breath.

When very active, polar bears use too much energy

Polar bears are the largest predators that live on land.

and tire easily. Running even a short distance causes overheating. To correct this problem, a quick dip in icy waters brings body temperature back to normal.

The coat of a polar bear is so good at keeping the animal warm that it can stretch out in the snow and take a nap!

Chapter Three

The Ice Bear

It is September and pack ice is forming on the Beaufort Sea north of Canada and Alaska. A female polar bear gluts herself with food. She knows by **instinct** that she is pregnant and needs the extra fat to survive **hibernation.** Soon, she will dig a birthing den in a snowdrift on the sea ice.

This expectant mother has gained nearly 160 kilograms (350 pounds). Most females weigh between 180 to 320 kilograms (400 to 700 lbs). Our mother-to-be now weighs 430 kilograms (950 lbs). The excess weight is almost all fat. She tunnels into the snow and creates a den, complete with a breathing hole for fresh air.

Only pregnant female polar bears hibernate. They do not fall into a deep sleep during hibernation. Their hearts beat more slowly—twenty-seven times per minute compared to the normal forty-six beats per minute. They do not need to eat or drink because their bodies feed off their excess fat.

Our young mother bear gives birth to twins in early January. The babies weigh about 0.5 kilogram (1 lb) each.

Would You Believe?
Six out of ten polar bear cubs die within their first year. Once a bear becomes an adult, the only **predator** to worry about is man. Adult polar bears live about twenty years in the wild—and forty years in a zoo.

The newborns nuzzle up to mother to nurse. By the time the family leaves the den in late March, the cubs have gained 11 kilograms (25 lbs). Mother bear has lost more than 136 kilograms (300 lbs). The cubs will stay with mom for the first two or three years of their lives.

During that time, mother teaches her babies how to hunt. She protects them from predators, including male polar bears. Because mothers keep cubs with them so long, they only give birth every three or four years.

Polar bears are mainly carnivores, or meat eaters. Young polar bears must learn where to find food. When ringed seals are plentiful, the bears eat only ringed seal blubber and leave the meat. Arctic foxes and glaucous gulls will clean up the leftovers.

But bears cannot rely on eating only ringed seals. They also feed on other kinds of seals, small whales, walruses, and narwhals. Polar bears will also hunt and eat reindeer, small rodents, seabirds, ducks, fish, and eggs. When really hungry, polar bears will even eat seaweed, berries, and garbage.

When the cubs turn three, the mother forces them to leave her. They are now **subadults**—too young to produce young and too old to stay with their mother. Many subadults hunt in small groups. It is more productive and safer. By the time polar bears are subadults, their only enemies are large male bears and humans.

If you were inside a polar bear den, your view of the outside world would look something like this.

A polar bear feeds on a whale carcass.

Would You Believe?
Polar bears have forty-two teeth. They use their front teeth to tear food apart. Their molars have jagged ridges that help them chew tough blubber.

Males polar bears live lonely lives. They travel across vast territories by themselves. Their days are spent hunting and resting. A male polar bear weighs between 400 and 720 kilograms (880 and 1,600 lbs). From black nose to stumpy tail, he measures 2.4 to 3 meters (8 to 10 feet), about 0.6 meter (2 ft) longer than females. It takes plenty of food to keep that hunting machine active.

In the southern regions of the polar bears' range, they sometimes live and feed in groups. At Churchill, Manitoba, Canada, for example, bears scavenge garbage dumps for food. Occasionally, along the Arctic coastlines, a dead whale washes ashore. The first polar bear on the scene "owns" the carcass. Other bears wanting to feed approach low to the ground. They show a **submissive** attitude. They circle the carcass, then meet the owner nose-to-nose. Only then will other bears be allowed to feed.

On rare occasions, a group of bears will actually hunt together. Once, pack ice trapped a **pod** of beluga whales. The whales breathed at a polynya. Male polar bears gathered round, waiting for the whales to surface. The group hunt was a great success. During the months the whales were trapped, the bears caught and hauled out more than forty whales. For the polar bears, beluga blubber was a feast!

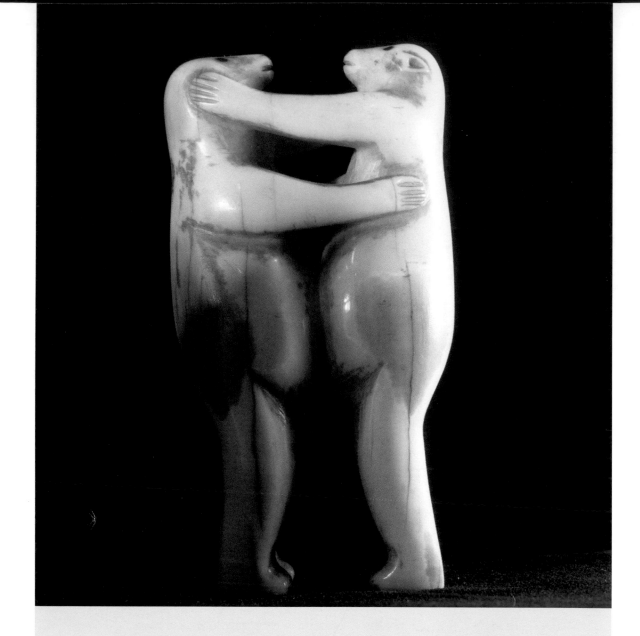

WHAT ARE POLAR BEARS CALLED IN DIFFERENT CULTURES?

Culture	Name	Meaning
Greenland	Tomassuk	Master of helping spirits
Inuit	Nanuk	Polar or ice bear
Inuit (poetry)	Pihoqahiak	Ever wandering one
Ket (Siberia)	Gyp or qoi	Grandfather or stepfather
Norwegian	Isbjørn	Ice bear
Russian	Beliy medved	White bear

An Inuit carving of polar bears from the 1800s shows the polar bears standing on two legs and looking a lot like humans.

Chapter Four

One Species, Many Cousins

There is only one polar bear species: *Ursus maritimus,* the sea bear. They live in distinct population groups, and the size of individual polar bears varies greatly. Size differences may be a result of food supplies or **genetics.** Smaller bear parents tend to have smaller bear cubs—just as shorter human parents tend to have shorter children.

Polar bear tracks have been spotted as far north as near the North Pole. Their southern range depends greatly on how much pack ice exists in a year. In a heavy ice year, polar bears travel as far south as the Pribilof Islands in the Bering Sea, Kamchatka Peninsula in Russia, and the Canadian province of Newfoundland and Labrador.

Polar bears live in only five nations: the United States, Canada, Greenland, Norway, and Russia. The world population ranges from 22,000 to 27,000 bears.

Would You Believe?
In a heavy ice year, polar bears walk from Greenland to Iceland—which causes quite a stir in Icelandic cities. Icelanders are not happy to have polar bears walking their streets.

A polar bear sleeps through a snowstorm in a shallow den.
Polar bears are perfectly suited to their cold, snowy habitat.

It is difficult to get an accurate count because bears move all the time.

Scientists believe that 60 percent of all polar bears live in Canada. The populations rise and fall depending on factors such as food supplies, human hunting, and pollution. Recently, the population in the Baffin Bay/Davis Strait region of Canada has decreased, while the Beaufort Sea population has grown.

Polar bears prefer their Arctic habitat to any other: sea ice, frigid waters, people-free islands, and northern coastlines. Although temperatures may drop to −51°Celsius (−60°Fahrenheit), polar bears do not feel cold. If a blizzard comes, bears dig shallow dens, curl up, and sleep through it.

POLAR BEAR RELATIVES: THE URSUS FAMILY

Polar bears belong to the genus *Ursus*. They have several relatives: brown bears, black bears, Malayan sun bears, and sloth bears. Of these four species, brown bears are closest to polar bears.

Most people know brown bears as grizzly bears and Kodiak bears. They live in Alaska, the northernmost

Main Polar Bear Populations
- The Beaufort Sea (northern and northwestern Alaska, northwestern Canada)
- The Canadian Arctic
- Central Siberia
- The Chukchi Sea (Wrangel Island, western Alaska)
- Greenland
- Spitzbergen/Franz Josef Land

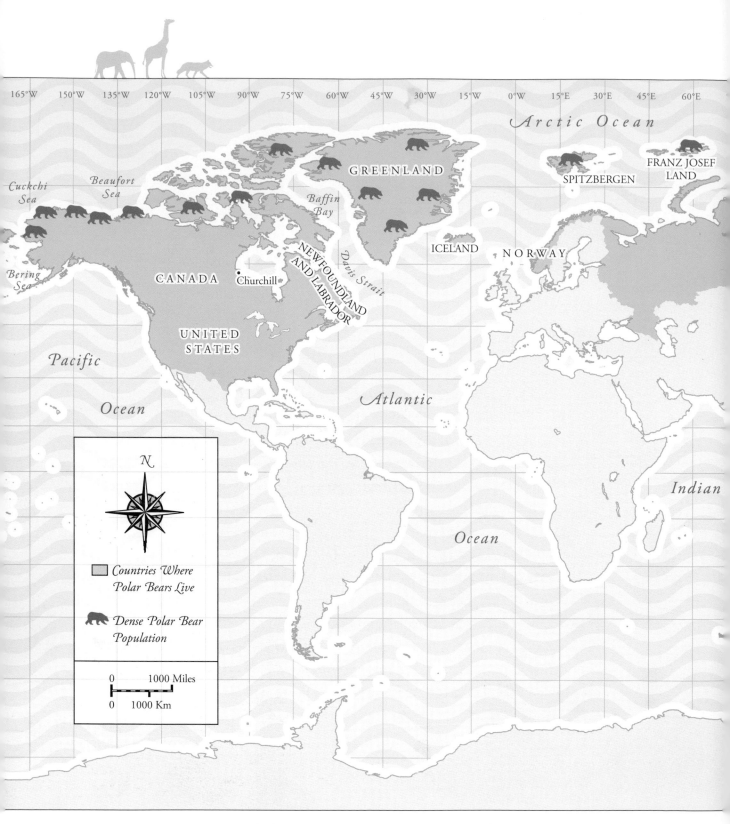

Polar bears live in the icy northern regions of the United States,
Canada, Russia, Greenland, and Norway.

Rocky Mountain states, and Canada. Europe and Asia have very small, isolated brown bear populations. Brown bears are similar in size to polar bears: 136 to 386 kilograms (300 to 850 lbs) and 2.7 to 3 meters (9 to 10 ft) long.

Brown bears are true omnivores. They eat both plants and animals, although most of their diet is berries, nuts, roots, and grasses. They also eat honey, eggs, insects, and carrion. In late summer, brown bears living near streams gorge themselves on salmon.

There are two types of black bears: American black bears and Asiatic black bears. The American version is smaller, weighing about 60 to 273 kilograms (132 to 600 lbs) and measuring about 1.2 to 1.8 meters (4 to 6 ft).

American black bears live where brown bears are not common. In a bear fight over territory, the grizzly will

Would You Believe?
Polar bears and brown bears are close cousins. They can breed together and produce healthy cubs.

win. The American black bear is not always black. Its color runs from a cinnamon brown to black. A pale blue version of the American black bear is called a glacier bear, and a white version is called a Kermode bear. Although they are white, Kermode bears are definitely not polar bears. They could not survive in the Arctic.

American black bears live in thirty-two of the fifty United States, Canada, and northern Mexico. They are also omnivores and eat everything from berries to insects, young deer to carrion, and salmon in the late summer.

Asiatic black bears are black, except for cream-colored patches on their chests. They live in northern India, Korea, Japan, Russia, and southern Asia. These bears eat fruits, bees' nests, rodents, and carrion. Adult males range from 100 to 200 kilograms (220 to 440 lbs). The females are about half the size of males, weighing in at 50 to 125 kilograms (110 to 275 lbs).

Malayan sun bears are the smallest bears. Adult bears weight up to 64 kilograms (140 lbs). They are named for the crescent-shaped patch of white or yellow fur on their chests. The rest of their fur is black. Malayan sun bears live in the tropical rain forests of Southeast Asia.

The strangest polar bear relatives are sloth bears. Sloth bears have dark fur with whitish snouts and white

Black bears are omnivores and will eat plants and animals. In late summer, black bears in Alaska enjoy gorging on blueberries.

and yellow patches on their chests. They seem to be miss-
ing a couple of upper teeth, but that is natural. Sloths are
termite eaters and suck the insects through the gap.

*Malayan sun bears are most active at night. They can often
be found resting on tree branches during the day.*

Chapter Five

The Past, The Present, and The Future

Nearly 100,000 years ago, polar bears roamed the frigid Arctic tundra. Fossils prove that polar bears existed even before that time. Many scientists believe that polar bears evolved from brown bears. Their bodies changed to suit their Arctic environment.

Humans living in the Arctic have always hunted polar bears. Remains of hunting sites date early hunts at 2,500 to 3,000 years ago. Those hunts had little impact on polar bear populations. They were individual or small group efforts, taking a few hundred bears each year. The loss was quickly replaced by the births of new cubs.

From 1500 to 1700, polar bear hunts became big business. Commercial hunts did not use all the bear parts as the Native peoples did. The skins were kept, but the meat and bones were thrown away.

Powerful rifles and snowmobiles almost brought

An Inuit family relaxes in an igloo in Canada's Northwest Territories. Because they are Native people, the Inuit are allowed to hunt polar bears.

the polar bear population to **extinction.** By the 1970s, it looked as though polar bears would survive only in zoos. That's when the five polar bear nations got together and banned sport hunting or random hunting of polar bears. Russia and Norway prohibit polar bear hunting, while Greenland, the United States, and Canada limit hunting to Native people. The international agreement requires these nations to protect birthing sites and migration trails and share polar bear research.

The United States passed the Marine Mammal Protection Act (MMPA) in 1972. This act covers polar bears, as well as seals, sea lions, walruses, whales, and dolphins. The MMPA prohibits taking or importing marine mammals for any reason. The one exception to the law is that Native people can hunt for **subsistence** purposes. The law has been very effective.

Populations of marine mammals have increased to healthy numbers. Species that had been endangered or threatened have been saved from extinction.

THREATS TO SURVIVAL

Polar bears stand at the top of the Arctic food chain. They are sentries of survival. When polar bear populations

Pollution is harmful to bears. Eating garbage may expose these bears to poisons that will make them sick.

decrease or the bears themselves become sickly or under-weight, something is wrong in the environment.

One major factor affecting polar bears today is global warming. While it might be hard to imagine, the Arctic tundra can be too warm for the polar bears. For the past several decades, the pack ice that the bears need for hunting has been melting a few weeks earlier every year—earlier than it did 100 years ago. Each week of less pack ice equals 10 kilograms (20 lbs) less weight on the bears. This is particularly difficult on new mothers that have lost about one-third of their body weight while denning. If they can't eat enough to make up for this lost weight, they may starve to death.

Pollution also hurts polar bears. Many Norwegian polar bears have high levels of poisonous chemicals in their systems. Every time they feed on tainted food, they take poison into their bodies. Sooner or later, the bears will die from these poisons. It is also possible that they will produce fewer **offspring** or offspring that cannot have young.

Oil spills add to the problems. Rich oil deposits in the northern part of the hemisphere encourage mining. However, spills cause serious damage. Oil on polar bear fur takes away the fur's ability to keep the bear warm. Spills also kill off or reduce food supplies. A major spill

in the Prudhoe Bay area of Alaska could seriously damage the Beaufort Sea bear population.

Scientists are aware of potential threats to polar bear populations. They work to reduce threats to the bears and increase the survival rate of bears in the wild. With human help, the great "ice bear" will roam the Arctic for many years to come.

Would You Believe?
Today's zoos provide polar bears with waterfalls, chilled swimming pools, snow machines, and puzzles. A typical polar bear puzzle is a fish in a large ice cube. Bears enjoy figuring out how to get the fish out of the ice.

Scientists and others are working to help ensure that polar bears survive and thrive in the future.

Glossary

extinction (ek-STINGK-shun) the state of no longer existing

genetics (juh-NEH-tiks) the study of how characteristics are passed on from one generation to the next through genes

hibernation (hy-burr-NAY-shun) the state of sleeping through the winter

ice pack (EYESS PAK) an expanse of pack ice

infrared (in-fruh-RED) light that is outside the visible spectrum

instinct (IN-stingkt) an inborn pattern of behavior

offspring (OFF-spring) the young of a species

pack ice (PAK EYESS) a mass of sea ice

pod (POD) a group of animals, such as whales

predator (PRED-uh-tur) an animal that hunts and kills other animals for food

sinew (SIN-you) a strong fiber that connects muscle to bone; tendon

subadults (SUB-uh-duhlts) not fully grown; like human teenagers

submissive (sub-MIH-siv) yielding to one who is stronger or has more authority

subsistence (sub-SIHS-tuhnss) the actions necessary to stay alive

tundra (TUHN-druh) a treeless plain in arctic regions in which the soil is permanently frozen

For More Information

Watch It

The Great White Bear, Video (Washington, D.C.: National Geographic, 1999)

World's Last Great Places: Arctic Kingdom, Life at the Edge, Video (Washington, D.C.: National Geographic, 1996)

Read It

Cotton, Jacqueline S. *Polar Bears.* Minneapolis: Lerner Publications, 2004.

Hall, Eleanor J. *Polar Bears.* San Diego: KidHaven Press, 2002.

Patent, Dorothy Hinshaw. *A Polar Bear Biologist at Work.* Danbury, Conn.: Franklin Watts, 2001.

Penny, Malcolm. *Polar Bear: Habitats, Life Cycles, Food Chains, Threats.* Austin, Tex.: Raintree Steck-Vaughn, 2000.

Look It Up

Visit our home page for lots of links about polar bears: *http://www.childsworld.com/links*

Note to Parents, Teachers, and Librarians: We routinely verify our Web links to make sure they are safe, active sites—so encourage your readers to check them out!

The Animal Kingdom
Where Do Polar Bears Fit In?

Kingdom: Animal

Phylum: Chordates (animals with backbones)

Class: Mammalia (animals that feed their young milk)

Order: Carnivora (meat-eating animals)

Family: Ursidae

Genus: *Ursus*

Species: *maritimus*

Index

About the Author

Sophie Lockwood is a former teacher and a longtime writer. She writes textbooks, newspaper articles, and magazine articles. Sophie enjoys writing about animals and their habits. The most interesting part of her research, Sophie says, is learning how scientists apply their knowledge to save endangered species. She lives with her husband in the foothills of the Blue Ridge Mountains.